Alfred's Basic Piano Library

Piano

Lesson Book
Level 4

A General MIDI disk (8556) and a Compact Disc (14549) are available, which include a full piano recording and background accompaniment.

*Teacher's discretion.

Willard A. Palmer • Morton Manus • Amanda Vick Lethco

Alfred Music
P.O. Box 10003
Van Nuys, CA 91410-0003
alfred.com

Third Edition
Copyright © MM by Alfred Music
All rights reserved. Produced in USA.

ISBN-10: 0-7390-0905-2
ISBN-13: 978-0-7390-0905-5

Illustrations by David Silverman (Painted by Cheryl Hennigar)

TARANTELLAS are always in quick $\frac{3}{8}$ or $\frac{6}{8}$ time. There are many popular piano pieces and songs that use this title. There are two stories about the origin of the *tarantella*. One is that this kind of music was played for a dance that originated in Taranto, Italy. Another is that the dance got its name from a very large spider, the tarantula, the bite of which was supposed to cause frenzied dancing. There was a superstition that dancing the tarantella was a cure for the poison of the tarantula. *Tarantellas* are always very tuneful, and are exciting to play.

Tarantella

You are now ready to begin RECITAL and THEORY BOOKS, Level 4.

D.C. al ✛, then Coda*

Coda

*Go back to the beginning and play to the sign ✛; then play the *Coda.*

4

Eighth Note Triplets

When three notes are grouped together with a figure *3* above or below the notes,
the group is called a **TRIPLET**.

The THREE NOTES of an

EIGHTH NOTE TRIPLET GROUP = ONE QUARTER NOTE.

When a piece contains triplets, count "TRIP-A-LET"
or "ONE & THEN"
or any way suggested by your teacher.

Practice these warm-ups before playing the next piece.

Haunted House

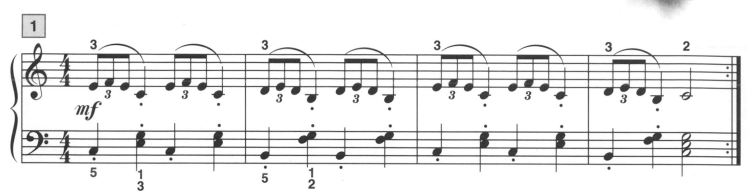

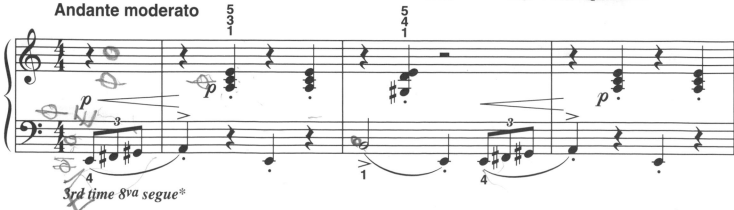

3rd time 8va segue*

SEGUE means *continuing* (to the end, or until further instructions appear).

You are now ready to begin EAR TRAINING and TECHNIC BOOKS, Level 4.

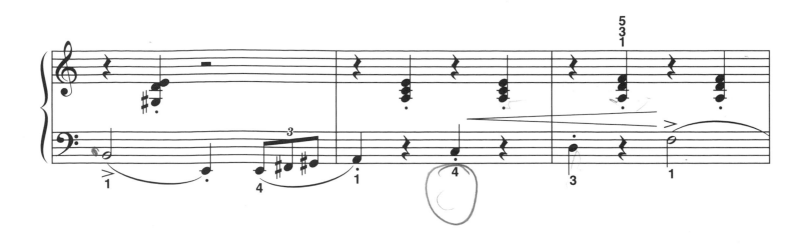

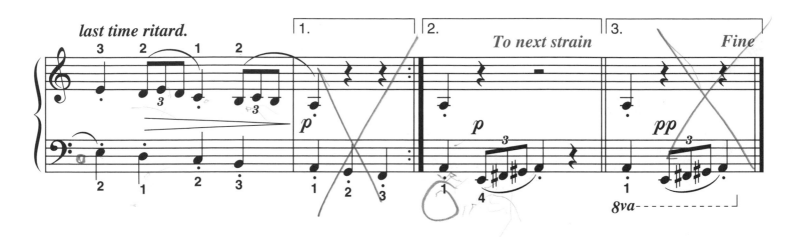

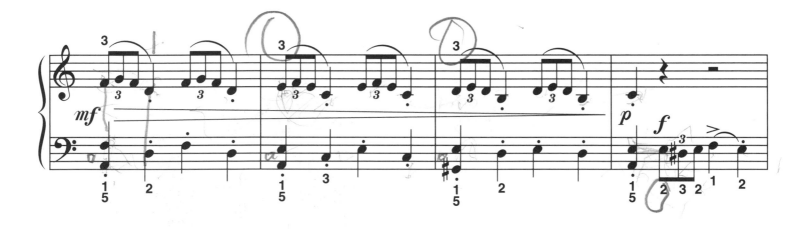

6

Triads: The 1st Inversion

Any **ROOT POSITION TRIAD** may be INVERTED
by moving the ROOT to the TOP.

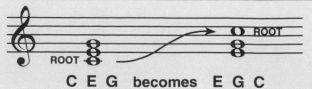

C E G becomes E G C

**All LETTER NAMES are the same, but the ROOT is on TOP.
This is called the FIRST INVERSION.**

1st Inversion Triads in C

Play with RH.   Use 1 2 5 on each triad.

Play the above with LH ONE OCTAVE LOWER. Use 5 3 1 on each triad.

In the 1st inversion, the ROOT is always
the TOP note of the INTERVAL of a **4th!**

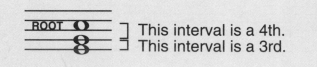

This interval is a 4th.
This interval is a 3rd.

Draw an arrow to the ROOT of each of the following triads.
   If there is an interval of a 4th in the triad, the TOP note of the 4th is the ROOT.
   If there is no 4th, the LOWEST note is the ROOT.

Play with RH.

The Hokey-Pokey

Slow rock tempo

Traditional

All of the chords in this piece are 1st inversion triads except three.
Find those three and name them before you play.

LH staccato

8

ARPEGGIATED CHORDS

When a wavy line appears beside a chord, the chord is *arpeggiated* (broken or rolled). Play the lowest note first, and quickly add the next higher notes one at a time until the chord is complete. The first note is played on the beat.

Prelude in A Minor

Andante moderato

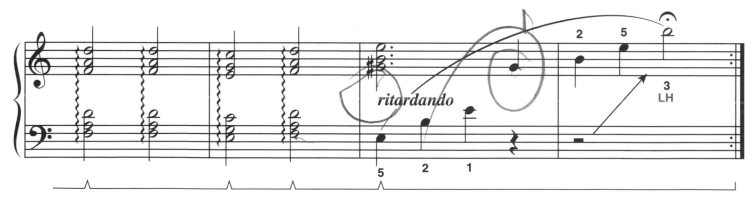

* Simile means in the same manner. In this case, continue playing triplets even though the **3**'s do not appear over or under the three-note groups.

poco ritardando - - - - - - - - - *a tempo*

poco ritardando - - - - - - - - - *a tempo*

ritardando

1.

2. *Play 3 times:* 1. Both hands *8va*
   2. As written, SLOWER
   3. Both hands *8va* lower, MUCH SLOWER

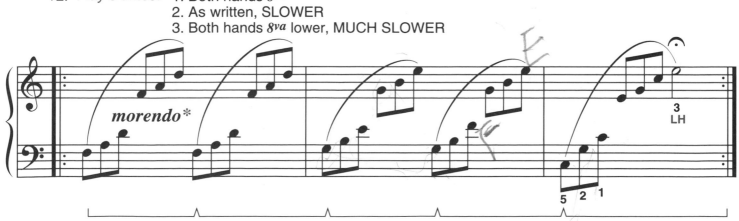

morendo*

* *Morendo* means "dying away."

Triads: The 2nd Inversion

Any **1st INVERSION TRIAD** may be inverted again
by moving the LOWEST NOTE to the TOP.

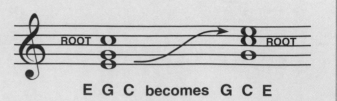

E G C becomes G C E

**All LETTER NAMES are the same, but the ROOT is in the MIDDLE.
This is called the SECOND INVERSION.**

2nd Inversion Triads in C

Play with LH.   Use 5 2 1 on each triad.

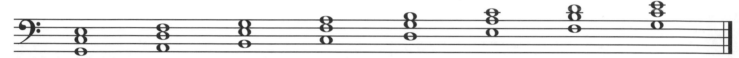

Play the above with RH ONE OCTAVE HIGHER. Use 1 3 5 on each triad.

In the 2nd inversion, the ROOT is always
the TOP note of the INTERVAL of a **4th!**

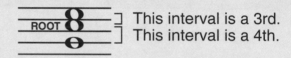

This interval is a 3rd.
This interval is a 4th.

Draw an arrow to the ROOT of each of the following triads.

If there is an interval of a 4th in the triad, the TOP note of the 4th is the ROOT.
If there is no 4th, the LOWEST note is the ROOT.

Play with RH.

REMEMBER: If the root is on the *bottom,* the triad is in **ROOT POSITION.**
If the root is on the *top,* the triad is in the **1st INVERSION.**
If the root is in the *middle,* the triad is in the **2nd INVERSION.**

Play the last line of music above with the RH, saying:

"ROOT POSITION, 1st INVERSION, 2nd INVERSION," etc., as you play.

Space Shuttle Blues

Play the LH alone first, naming the root of each triad.
Every LH chord is a 2nd inversion triad, so the root is always the MIDDLE note!

*Play the pairs of eighth notes a bit unevenly, long-short.
**Notice that the time signature changes for one measure only.

Olympic Procession

Each LH chord in this piece, and every
RH 3-note chord, is a 2nd inversion triad!

*The time signature 𝄴 indicates COMMON TIME, which is the same as $\frac{4}{4}$ time.

Triads in All Positions

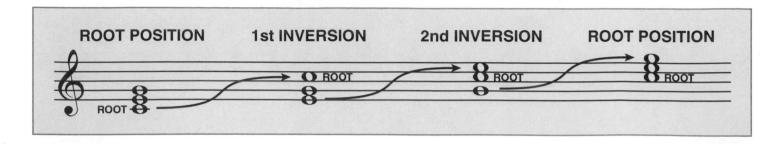

Play the following:

C MAJOR TRIAD

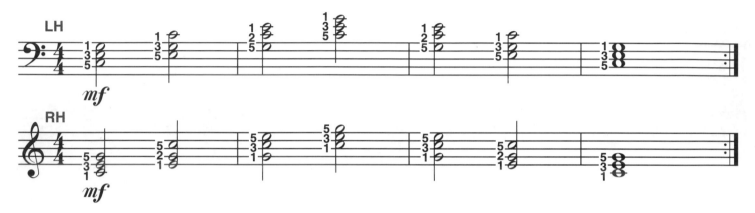

G MAJOR TRIAD

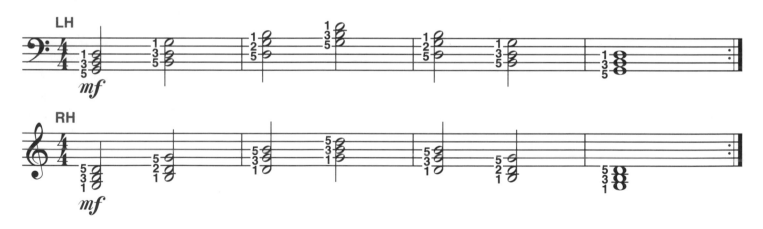

The same, beginning one octave higher:

IMPORTANT! Repeat all of the above,
using ARPEGGIATED CHORDS:

 *etc.*

Farewell to Thee (Aloha Oe)

"Aloha Oe" is used in the Hawaiian Islands as a greeting or farewell. This well-known song, which is played and sung for tourists arriving and leaving the Islands, was composed by the last queen of the Hawaiian Islands, Lydia Kamekaha Liliuokalani, who reigned in 1891–1893.

Adagio

Queen L. K. Liliuokalani

Black Forest Polka

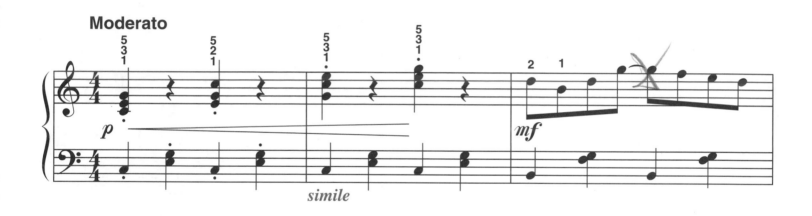

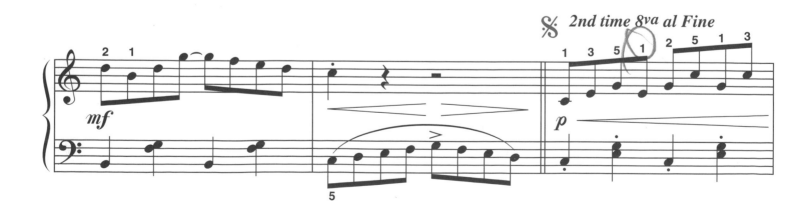

simile

p

mf

Fine

D.S. ℅ al Fine

* **D.S. (Dal Segno)** means *from the sign.*

   D.S. ℅ al Fine means *repeat from the sign ℅ and play to the FINE.*

Major Scales in Parallel Motion

When the hands move in the same direction, ascending or descending, it is called PARALLEL MOTION.

In the C, G & D MAJOR scales in parallel motion, LH & RH 3's always play together;
4's always play next to the KEY note.

Play hands separately, then together. Play slowly at first, then gradually increase speed.

Circled finger numbers are the same in both hands!

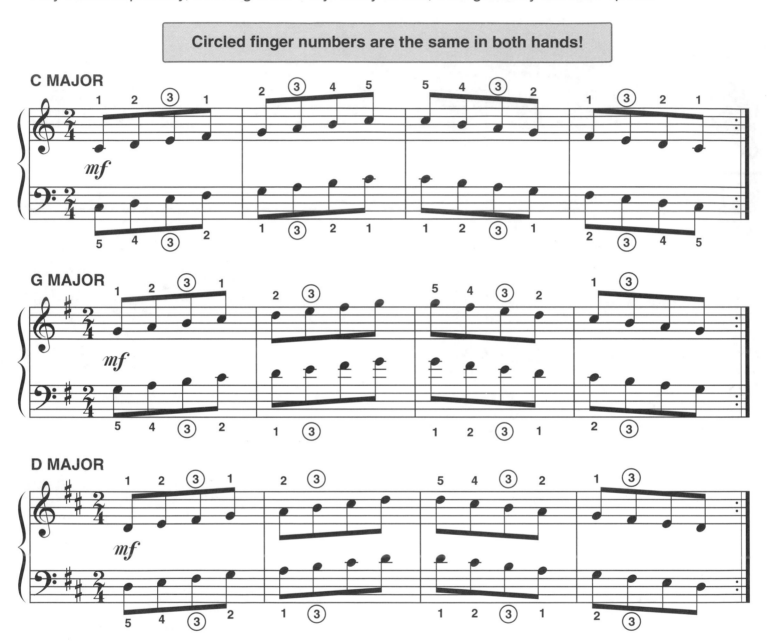

In the F MAJOR scale, the THUMBS of the RH and LH play together (except on the first and last notes of the scale). RH 4 plays B♭. RH 5 NEVER PLAYS!

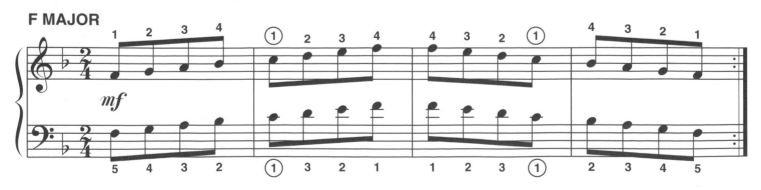

19

Notes played between the main beats of a measure and
held across the beat are called SYNCOPATED NOTES.

In the following rhythm, the first quarter note is SYNCOPATED:

COUNT: 1 & 2 & 3 & 4 &

See how many syncopated notes you can find in this piece!

Calypso Holiday!

Two-Part Writing

In some music, one hand must play two melodies that have notes of different time values, at the same time.

1st or principal part (the melody)

Play with RH.

2nd part (counter-melody)

Play with RH.

When both parts are written on ONE staff, the note-stems of the UPPER melody are turned UP, and the note-stems of the LOWER melody are turned DOWN. This is called TWO-PART WRITING.

Play with RH.

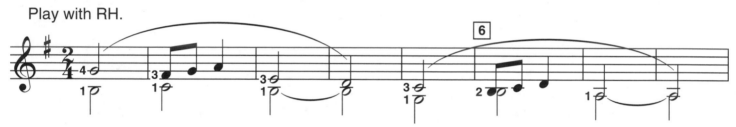

In the 6th measure, the upper (1st) part begins with the eighth note B. The lower (2nd) part has the same B, but it is a half note. Play the B only once, and hold it for the value of the half note while the upper melody continues.

In the 7th and 8th measures, both parts are the same. In this case the note is given two stems, but it is played only once.

Processional from
Pomp and Circumstance No. 1

This is one of the most famous of all melodies. It is often played
for royal coronation celebrations and graduation ceremonies.

Molto maestoso*

Sir Edward Elgar

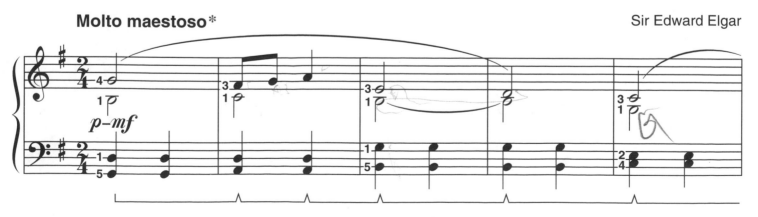

*Molto means "very." *Molto maestoso* means "very majestically."

Allargando means "broadening." It means an increased dignity of style, slowing the tempo while maintaining or increasing volume.

The Complete Seventh Chord Vocabulary

Play each of the following seventh chords.

Say the note names as you play.

Stems up = RH
Stems down = LH

A C E G

B D F A

C E G B

D F A C

E G B D

F A C E

G B D F

With this vocabulary you can play seventh chords in any key, simply by using the key signature.

MEMORIZE the Complete Seventh Chord Vocabulary.

Seventh Chord Review

A SEVENTH CHORD may be formed by adding to the ROOT POSITION TRIAD a note that is a 7th above the ROOT.

The four notes of a seventh chord are:

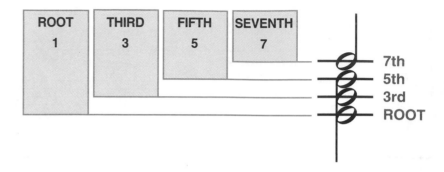

Seventh chords in ROOT POSITION (with ROOT at the BOTTOM) look like this:

The 5th is often omitted from the seventh chord. This makes it simple to play with one hand.

Play with LH:

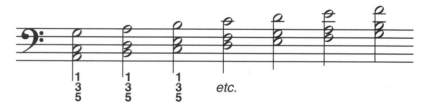

The 3rd is sometimes omitted.

Play with LH:

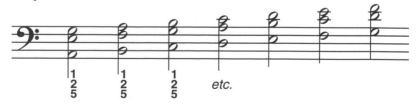

All seventh chords on this page are in ROOT POSITION!

REMEMBER: When the interval from the lowest note of the chord to the highest is a 7th, the BOTTOM NOTE is the ROOT!

Swinging Sevenths

Every LH chord in this piece is a seventh chord in root position! Play the LH alone at first.
Notice which seventh chords have the 5th omitted and which have the 3rd omitted.

Moderately slow, with a "swing feeling"

Inversions of Seventh Chords

Four-note seventh chords may be played in the following positions.
All note names are the same in each position, but in a different order!

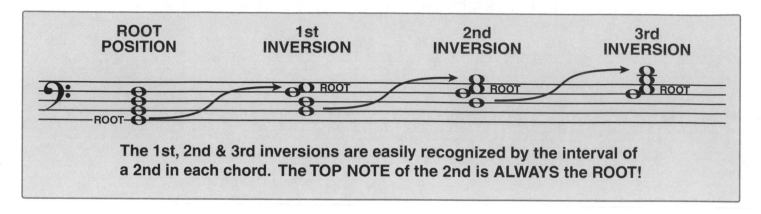

The 1st, 2nd & 3rd inversions are easily recognized by the interval of
a 2nd in each chord. The TOP NOTE of the 2nd is ALWAYS the ROOT!

Here are some seventh chords with omitted 5ths or 3rds.
Play the LH as written, then the RH one octave higher.

1. The G⁷ chord is the V⁷ chord in the key of C MAJOR. Its notes are **G B D F**.

5th (D) omitted:

3rd (B) omitted:

2. The D⁷ chord is the V⁷ chord in the key of G MAJOR. Its notes are **D F♯ A C**.

5th (A) omitted:

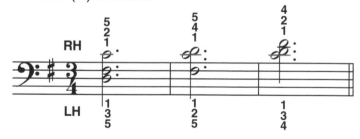

3rd (F♯) omitted:

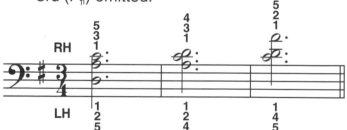

3. The C⁷ chord is the V⁷ chord in the key of F MAJOR. Its notes are **C E G B♭**.

5th (G) omitted:

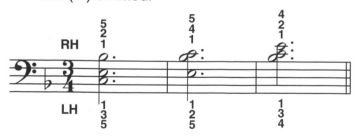

3rd (E) omitted:

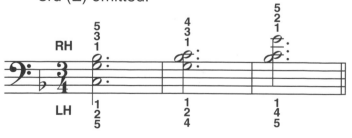

America, the Beautiful

Samuel A. Ward

Draw an arrow to the root of each seventh chord.

The Key of E Minor (Relative of G Major)

E MINOR is the relative of **G MAJOR**.

Both keys have the same key signature (1 sharp, F♯).
REMEMBER: The RELATIVE MINOR begins on the 6th tone of the MAJOR SCALE.

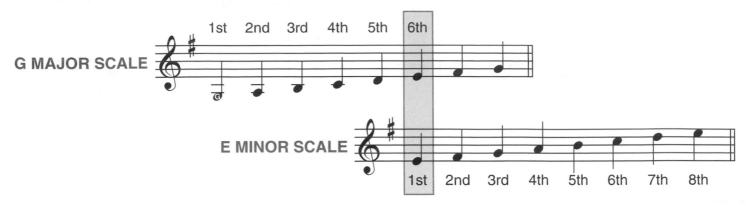

Practice each of the following scales, first with the RH, as written,
then with the LH, 2 octaves lower than written.

1. **THE NATURAL MINOR SCALE:** Use the same tones as the relative major scale.

2. **THE HARMONIC MINOR SCALE:** 7th (D) raised one half step ASCENDING & DESCENDING.

3. **THE MELODIC MINOR SCALE:** 6th (C) and 7th (D) raised one half step ASCENDING;
descends like natural minor.

The E Harmonic Minor Scale in Contrary Motion

Play several times daily!

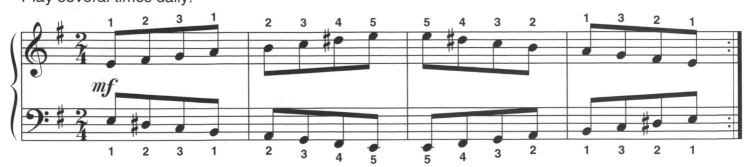

The E NATURAL MINOR and MELODIC MINOR scales may also be played in contrary motion.

The House of the Rising Sun

KEY OF E MINOR
Key signature: 1 sharp (F♯)

Andante moderato
2nd time both hands 8va segue

legato

mf

Ped. simile

RH

The Primary Chords in E Minor

Reviewing the E MINOR SCALE, LH ascending.

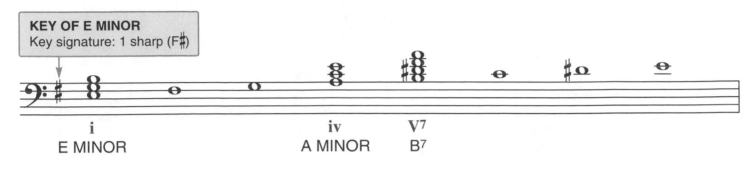

i		**iv**	**V⁷**	
E MINOR		A MINOR	B⁷	

The following positions are often used
for smooth progressions:

i   iv   V⁷
E MINOR   A MINOR   B⁷

E MINOR PROGRESSION with broken i, iv & V⁷ chords.
Play several times with LH.

E MINOR i, iv & V⁷ chords in all positions.
Play several times with RH.

Waves of the Danube

Ivanovici
Special arrangement by P.M.L.

Moderate waltz tempo

Sixteenth Notes

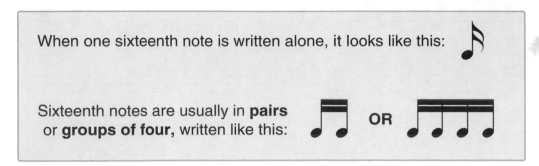

When one sixteenth note is written alone, it looks like this:

Sixteenth notes are usually in **pairs** or **groups of four,** written like this: **OR**

Four sixteenth notes are played in the time of **one quarter note.**

COUNT: 1 - a - & - a
or: Four six-teenth notes

There can be 16 sixteenth notes in one measure of **COMMON (4/4) TIME!**

Play several times: first ADAGIO, then ANDANTE, then ALLEGRO MODERATO.

Two sixteenth notes are played in the time of **one eighth note.**

Play several times: first ADAGIO, then ANDANTE, then ALLEGRO MODERATO.

Gypsy Dance

KEY OF E MINOR
Key signature: 1 sharp (F♯)

Andante moderato

Last time begin SLOWLY and play gradually faster and faster to the FINE.

Anna Magdalena Bach's notebook may be the most famous musical collection in the world. It was probably presented by Johann Sebastian Bach, one of the greatest musicians of all time, to his wife, Anna Magdalena, as a birthday present. It must have been a delight to the eye when it was new. The initials "A.M.B." and the date "1725" were stamped on the cover in gold. The book was green with gold borders, two locks and a red satin ribbon. In this book, the members of the Bach family were to write many of their favorite pieces. No one knows who actually composed this famous *MUSETTE.* It is in the handwriting of Anna Magdalena. In the original manuscript there are no indications of tempo, dynamics, fingering, phrasing, staccato, etc. These have all been added by the editor. This *MUSETTE* has been recorded by many celebrated keyboard artists.

Musette

From *ANNA MAGDALENA BACH'S NOTEBOOK*

D. C. al Fine

The Dotted Eighth Note

A DOTTED EIGHTH NOTE has the same value as an eighth note tied to a sixteenth note:

Count aloud and play:

Count: 1 a & a *etc.*

The following line should sound exactly the same as the line above it. The only difference is the way it is written.

Count: 1 a & a *etc.*

The Battle Hymn of the Republic

Steffe-Howe

Slow march tempo

Maestoso

36

The B♭ Major Scale

REMEMBER! The MAJOR SCALE is made of TWO TETRACHORDS joined by a WHOLE STEP.
The pattern of each tetrachord is: WHOLE STEP—WHOLE STEP—HALF STEP.

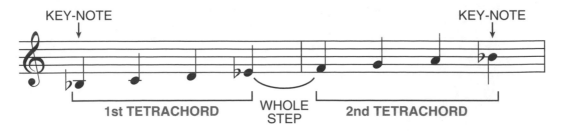

Beginning with LH 3, the scale is fingered in groups of 3 2 1 - 4 3 2 1. End on 3.

After beginning with RH 4, the fingering groups then fall 1 2 3 - 1 2 3 4. End on 4.

Notice that LH 4 plays E♭; RH 4 plays B♭. The 5th finger is not used in either hand!

Proceed to the following only after you have mastered the above!

HANDS TOGETHER in PARALLEL MOTION

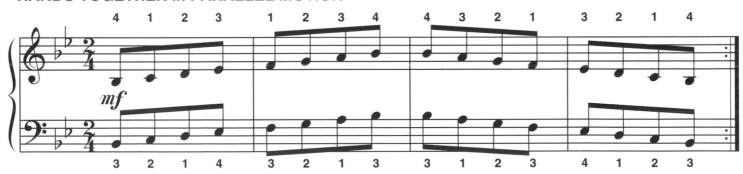

HANDS TOGETHER in CONTRARY MOTION

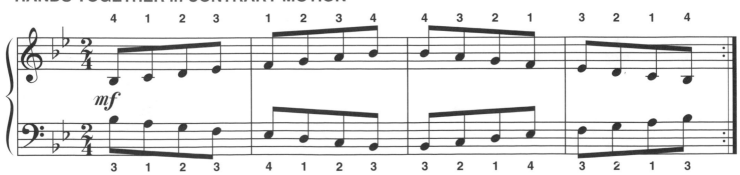

The Magic Piper

KEY OF B♭ MAJOR
Key signature: 2 flats (B♭ & E♭)

Allegro moderato

The Primary Chords in B♭ Major

Reviewing the B♭ MAJOR SCALE, LH ascending.

KEY OF B♭ MAJOR
Key signature: 2 flats (B♭ & E♭)

I
B♭ MAJOR

IV
E♭ MAJOR

V7
F7

The following positions are often used
for smooth progressions:

I
B♭ MAJOR

IV
E♭ MAJOR

V7
F7

Play with RH as written, then with LH one octave lower.

RH

LH

I   IV   I   V7 (5th omitted)   I   V7 (3rd omitted)   I

He's Got the Whole World in His Hands

Moderately and rhythmically

Spiritual

mf-pp

*Play pairs of eighth notes a bit unevenly, long-short.

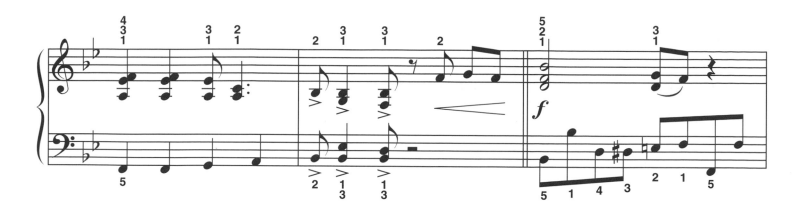

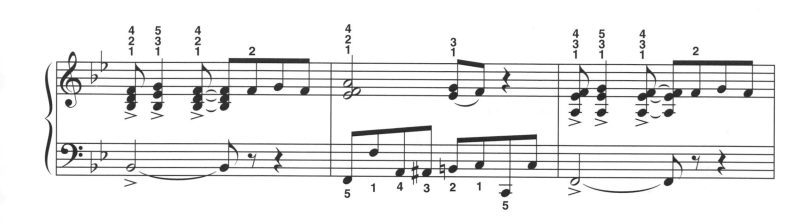

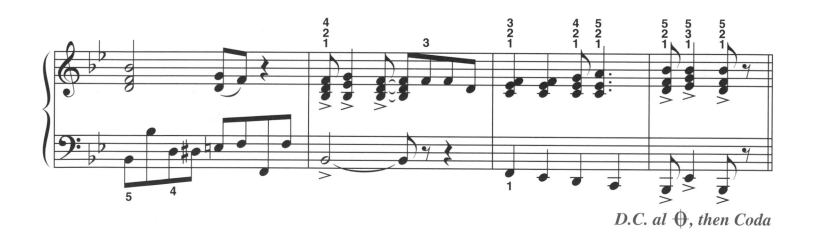

D.C. al 𝄌, then Coda

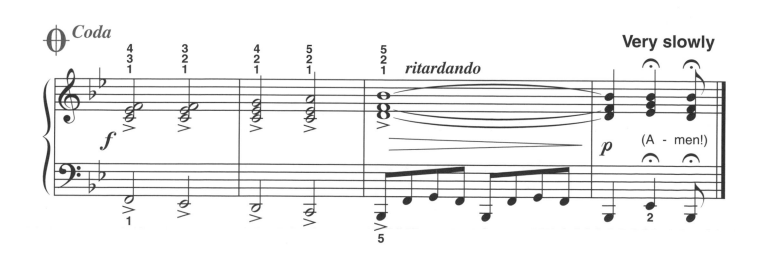

Coda

Very slowly

ritardando

(A - men!)

The Key of G Minor (Relative of B♭ Major)

G MINOR is the relative of **B♭ MAJOR**.

Both keys have the same key signature (2 flats, B♭ & E♭).
REMEMBER: The RELATIVE MINOR begins on the 6th tone of the MAJOR SCALE.

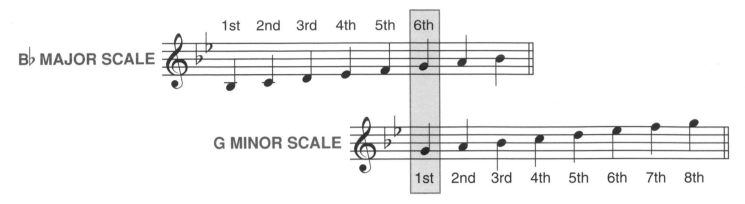

Practice each of the following scales, first with the RH, as written,
then with the LH, 2 octaves lower than written.

1. **THE NATURAL MINOR SCALE:** Use the same tones as the relative major scale.

2. **THE HARMONIC MINOR SCALE:** 7th (F) raised one half step ASCENDING & DESCENDING.

3. **THE MELODIC MINOR SCALE:** 6th (E♭) and 7th (F) raised one half step (to E♮ and F♯) ASCENDING;
   descends like the natural minor.

The G Harmonic Minor Scale in Contrary Motion

Play several times daily!

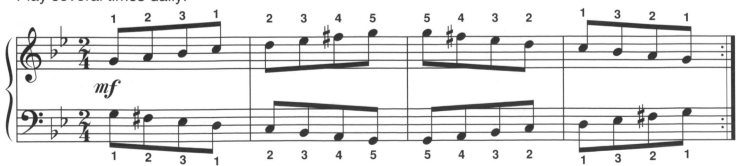

The G NATURAL MINOR and MELODIC MINOR scales may also be played in contrary motion.

Spinning Wheel

KEY OF G MINOR
Key signature: 2 flats (B♭ & E♭)

Allegro moderato

2nd time 8va

D. C. al ⊕, then CODA

The Primary Chords in G Minor

Reviewing the G MINOR SCALE, LH ascending.

KEY OF G MINOR
Key signature: 2 flats (B♭ & E♭)

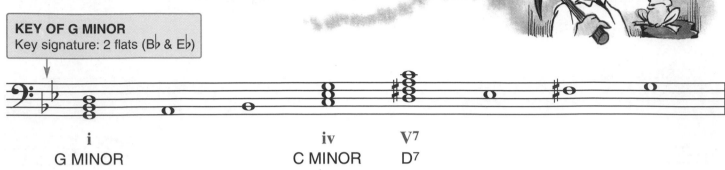

i   iv   V7
G MINOR   C MINOR   D7

The following positions are often used
for smooth progressions: The same, one octave higher.

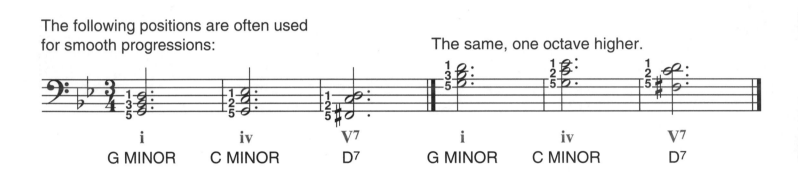

i   iv   V7   i   iv   V7
G MINOR   C MINOR   D7   G MINOR   C MINOR   D7

G MINOR PROGRESSION with broken **i**, **iv** & **V7** chords.

Play several times.

INVERSIONS OF V7 (D7) CHORDS with 5th (A) omitted.

Play several times.   The same, broken. Play several times.

The third line of this piece is in B♭ MAJOR, the relative of G minor. The primary chords are reviewed with the same positions in RH and LH. The fourth line returns to G minor, with the primary chords of that key also in the same positions in RH and LH.

Waltz in G Minor

> **KEY OF G MINOR**
> Key signature: 2 flats (B♭ & E♭)

Waltz tempo

D. C. al Fine

Harmonic Minor Scales in Parallel Motion

In the scales on this page, LH & RH 3's play together; 4's play next to the KEY note.

Play hands separately, then together. Play slowly at first, then gradually increase speed.

Circled finger numbers are the same in both hands!

The NATURAL & MELODIC MINOR SCALES may also be practiced in parallel motion. The fingering is the same.

Blow, Winds, Blow!

(A Pirate Song)

Repeated-Note Warm-Ups

Master these two warm-ups thoroughly before proceeding to *COMEDIANS' DANCE.*

Practice very slowly at first.
As each warm-up is mastered, it may be played faster.

Comedians' Dance

Dmitri Kabalevsky

Fine

(still 8va)

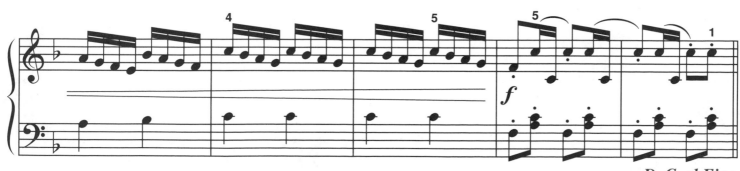

D. C. al Fine

Certificate of Promotion

This is to certify that

has successfully completed Level 4
of the LESSON BOOK and is hereby promoted
to Level 5 of Alfred's Basic Piano Library.

Date _____

Teacher _____